T0243749

Praise for *The Art of Good Deeds*

"Doing good doesn't have to be something big. Helping little old ladies like myself or just giving a smile to someone are good deeds we all can do."

—**Opal Lee,** retired teacher, counselor, activist known as the "grandmother of Juneteenth," and Nobel Peace Prize nominee

"The testimonials we read here show that good deeds are a lifestyle."

—**Melba Wilson**, Harlem-based restaurateur and owner of Melba's Restaurant, Food Network personality, president of the board of directors for the NYC Hospitality Alliance, and the author of *Melba's American Comfort: 100 Recipes from My Heart to Your Kitchen*

"We all need good deeds in our lives. This book shows that service is the greatest wealth we can transfer to others."

—**Chris Rey**, youngest elected mayor of Spring Lake, North Carolina, 36th International President of Phi Beta Sigma Fraternity, Inc., and president of Barber-Scotia College

"The generous souls who tell their stories in this book are an inspiration for all of us!"

—**DeMarco Morgan**, broadcast journalist at ABC News and co-anchor of *GMA3: What You Need to Know with Eva Pilgrim*

THE
Art of Good Deeds

Also by Dwayne Ashley

I'll Find a Way or Make One: A Tribute to Historically Black Colleges and Universities (Coauthored with Juan Williams)

Dream Internships! It's Not Who You Know . . . It's What You Know

Eight Winning Steps to Creating a Successful Special Event

THE
Art of Good Deeds

Dwayne Ashley
with Ava Williams Muhammad

BROADLEAF BOOKS
Minneapolis

THE ART OF GOOD DEEDS

Library of Congress Cataloging-in-Publication Data

Names: Ashley, Dwayne, editor.
Title: The art of good deeds / [edited by] Dwayne Ashley.
Description: Minneapolis : Broadleaf Books, [2024]
Identifiers: LCCN 2023058884 (print) | LCCN 2023058885
    (ebook) | ISBN 9781506488684 (hardback) |
    ISBN 9781506488691 (ebook)
Subjects: LCSH: Charity. | Generosity. | Humanitarianism. |
    Philanthropists.
Classification: LCC BJ1533.C36 A78 2024 (print) | LCC
    BJ1533.C36 (ebook) | DDC 177/.7—dc23/eng/20240104
LC record available at https://lccn.loc.gov/2023058884
LC ebook record available at https://lccn.loc.gov/2023058885

Cover image: Katarina Nskbsky
Cover design: Georgia Scott

Print ISBN: 978-1-5064-8868-4
eBook ISBN: 978-1-5064-8869-1

Printed in India.

Contents

INTRODUCTION

How many times have you heard the word "philanthropist" and the most immediate thought was a wealthy person who donated money to someone or to an organization in need? I don't normally define philanthropy as how much money you can give or how many checks you can write. As the CEO and founder of Bridge Philanthropic Consulting, I teach my clients about the psychology of giving. I tell them that true philanthropists aren't motivated by their name on a building but are driven by their emotions. Philanthropists wish to touch hearts and souls. They desire to make a difference, often because someone has made a difference in their lives.

You don't have to be rich to be a philanthropist. The measure of a good deed is not solely based on currency, but it stems from the two Greek words wonderfully woven within "philanthropy," which are "phila," meaning love, and "anthro," meaning man. The two words joined together perfectly define a philanthropist as someone who loves mankind.

So, how does a philanthropist spread love to mankind? It is very simple. They take care of the people around them through acts of kindness and good deeds. They know that doing a good deed is putting good energy into the universe and that it's the right thing to do.

Anyone can give. The elderly lady who pays her tithes every Sunday, giving ten percent of her Social Security check, is a philanthropist.

Philanthropy is giving without expecting something in return. Yet, because of the laws of nature, the energy that we put out always comes back to us. When you give, the universe will always take care of you.

Philanthropy is about being authentic in your actions. If you don't have a lot of money to give, you may still give in many meaningful ways. You may help an elderly person by calling an organization like Meals on Wheels to deliver meals to their home. Or you may help an older person who isn't tech savvy fill out forms online.

SERVICE AND GIVING BACK

Pay attention to ways that you can give that do not require you to write a check to an organization. When my cousin was a single mother of three children living in Houston and taking the bus, I purchased a car for her. In return, I made her promise that her children would receive an education and attend college, which they did. I think that one simple deed changed the trajectory of my cousin's life, as well as her children's.

You may always give in service. My ninety-year-old aunt was the pillar of her community and a beacon of light. When I went home for her homegoing, I saw the outpouring of good deeds and philanthropy. The community brought food every day. They cooked. They took care of our family. This is philanthropy at its best.

BIPOC (Black, Indigenous, and people of color) communities may not recognize preparing a meal for others as philanthropy. It is just what BIPOCs have traditionally done. Service to others in your community is philanthropy.

I grew up in a very giving community where the whole neighborhood helped to raise my siblings and me. All the children played with each other, and if our neighbors saw us doing something wrong, we would get it, and when our parents came home, we would get it again. Mr. Henry, who lived down the street, was a postal worker, but he also was a deacon at the church. My high school English teacher, Ms. Ida Collier, who also taught French and Spanish, was an amazing teacher and member of my extended family. She always did more than her job required. I was inspired by her commitment to young people. My mother was a den mother for the Scouts and a member of the Red Hat Society, which served as a support group for Black women. My community taught me that giving back was just what you had to do. Often, I witnessed my father stop and help women who had flat tires along the road. He wasn't looking for anything in return; he was serving the community. The deeds of my father taught my brothers and me the importance of giving back.

From my great-grandmother, I learned the importance of community and taking care of the people around me. My great-grandmother was a midwife. When families could not pay her, they often gave her portions of their land, which she in turn donated to create one of the first Black schools in Heflin, Louisiana. Eventually, the school became a church, which generations of my family and neighbors have attended to this day.

When I was a student at Wiley College, I joined Phi Beta Sigma fraternity. The brothers have always been there for me. Throughout my entire career, they have continued to honor, award, and support me. The brothers taught me that a Sigma man was committed to community service, excellence, and doing your personal best. These three commitments have served as a model for my entire life.

Often family philanthropy is not thought of as philanthropy, but I think it is. I am reminded of my older brother who left me an inheritance when he passed away in 2016. I started my business, Bridge Philanthropic Consulting, with the money my brother gave me. I thought he would have left everything to my mother, but he left a sizable estate to all of my siblings. It was a great deed that I didn't expect. I am grateful for my brother's seeds of goodness, which have allowed me to grow a diverse firm with a unique approach to philanthropy. It is an opportunity for me to change the perceptions of philanthropy.

TIME

Giving of time is also a charitable act. It provides the emotional support someone may need to navigate life. We have all had a friend who was devastated after a break-up. Sometimes, all we need to do is go to their home with a bottle of wine, sit down with them, and say, "I got you." Sometimes, all it takes is a simple phone call to give a person our time. During the COVID-19 crisis, a lot of my faith-based friends were barely hanging on by a thread and needed someone to check on them. We always look at our pastors and our priests as our go-to, but they are human and need our help as well. The experience opened me up in a different way and allowed me to realize that we need to take care of everybody. I now call my family pastor and my faith-based leader friends to check on them. I ask, "How are you doing? Are you taking care of yourself?" There was a huge increase of mental health issues during the pandemic, especially with Black men. I often call the men in my family and friends to ask if they are doing okay.

Mentoring is another opportunity to give. The great civil rights leader John Lewis was a mentor of mine. I was inspired by his love for this country and his love of service. Right now, I offer my time to entrepreneurs who want to start their own businesses.

Works of kindness inspire others to give. I am reminded of my grandfather's acts of goodness. He was a minimalist. He lived on a farm in a cabin with no running water. Part of his profoundness was his simplicity. His modest lifestyle taught me that happiness is not based on material things, but it is based on how you feel within and how you treat others. My grandfather did not have the opportunity to attend college, but he worked very hard and was passionate about being a farmer. Often, he would hire college students to work and stay on his farm during the summer. It was his way of giving back. The money the students earned was used to buy books and school supplies when they went back to school. My grandfather's good deeds inspired my passion for helping college students when I worked for the United Negro College Fund and the Thurgood Marshall Fund.

GIFTS TO SELF

Giving is definitely my love language, but it is equally important to reward myself. Traveling the world is a gift for me. I go on three to four trips per year, and I have visited over one hundred countries. I am inspired by meeting new people and learning about new cultures. I am also a strong advocate of self-care. If you are not physically, mentally, and spiritually well, how can you be the best for someone else? My go-to for self-care is burning candles. I also love to close my eyes to meditate and just breathe. Music is my medicine also. Artists such as Donna Sommer and Earth, Wind & Fire have aided in the healing of my soul. Good music makes me want to dance. Many of my Generation X friends are taking care of their elderly Baby Boomer parents and are neglecting themselves. I have pulled them aside and said, you are going to make yourself sick, so you need to take care of you.

Philanthropy means leaving a legacy. Legacy is the path that our soul needs to grow and live on past our time on earth. Maya Angelou said, "Philanthropy is the giving of your time, giving of your soul, but particularly giving of your soul and spirit." Legacy is an opportunity for the soul to continue to have an impact on generations to come. Some of the wealthiest families, like the Fords and Rockefellers, have a legacy which continues to be amplified because their souls have continued to live through their foundations and their philanthropic work. Others, like Ms. Opal Lee, the "Grandmother of Juneteenth" who dedicated her life to freedom, are less known. Her wit, enthusiasm, humor, and beautiful soul inspire me to do more. During a meeting, I once heard her pray: "God, I'm so grateful." The way she said "grateful" was powerful. I knew she was grateful to have seen all that she had seen in her ninety-six years.

I am grateful to you for you reading this book and for taking the time to discover that everyone, including you, has the power to be a philanthropist.

—Dwayne Ashley
New York, NY
2024

ONE

CHARITY BEGINS WITH FAMILY

Betty Aquino

I was born and raised in Harlem, New York. My parents came to this country from the Dominican Republic. Growing up, I would ask myself, Why don't organizations come to Harlem? I hoped that more financial literacy programs, job opportunities, mentors, and Fortune five hundred companies would come to Harlem. I have made a commitment to teaching the people in my community about financial literacy. For over eighteen years, I have worked in the financial industry because it is what I love to do. I've always had a passion for paying it forward, so I thought it made sense to use my financial literacy knowledge to serve my community. I give back by guiding young professionals

and through offering financial literacy to elementary students in East Harlem. I also served as a mentor to a woman I worked with who wanted to know how I navigated through corporate America. We have learned from each other.

To help women attorneys, I developed the Women in Leadership Networking & Career Development Group. The idea for the group came to me in 2017 when I was working at Esquire Bank. It was a male-dominated space. At times, I was the only female, and only female of color, sitting in the boardroom. There were joyful moments, and at the same time it was lonely. There weren't enough people who looked or sounded like me in leadership positions. When I first started the group, I thought only five women would show up, but to my surprise, forty-five women attended my first Women in Leadership event. There are now a number of companies that have incorporated women and leadership events into their programs. It is a space where women can network, exchange ideas, create synergies, and build long-lasting partnerships. I feel I have impacted the world with my Women in Leadership program.

I recently had a webinar and invited a major, well-known, well-respected attorney to participate. To my surprise, he said yes. I am in awe of those of his stature who give back. It showed me you're never too big to be humble. Despite all the money, accolades, and access he had, he still wanted to meet new people. His willingness to help others fascinated me.

Philanthropy is an exchange of kindness. When we exchange kindness, it brings respect and an increased level of appreciation. Good deeds come in many forms, done out of the kindness of the heart. I once mentioned to Dwayne that I picked up the bill for someone at the grocery store, and he said that was philanthropy. I thought I was just being kind to someone at the store, but that allowed me to broaden my view of philanthropy.

Although my giving is known in banking and legal services, I was inspired to give by my family. When my husband and I wanted to expand our family, our parents were very supportive of us. I've spent a lot of time giving back to my mom's congregation; she is pastor of a church that impacts her community in Providence, Rhode Island.

In July 2022, I lost my grandmother. The experience changed how I view time and giving back to the people I love. Before my grandmother passed, she was in a nursing home. My family and I had to fight really hard to get her out and move her to a brand-new renovated apartment. She was so happy. I enjoyed seeing the joy on her face every day. I learned from my grandmother that you don't have to be financially well off to give. Her passing made me want to look for ways to help other older adults. I admire the way the previous generation lived their lives—their family values and respect for elders.

I teach my kids about philanthropy. I want future generations of my family to build our legacy around philanthropy, and that starts with teaching them to treat people as they would want to be treated and that good behavior comes in different forms. I let them know how blessed they are and remind them of other people who are less fortunate. When we go back home to the Dominican Republic, they say, "Hey Ma, I want to take these clothes to give away." My kids are already giving back, spreading the love to others, doing good deeds.

GIFTS TO SELF

I give a lot, but I could give more. Me being me is my way of impacting the world. God made me as I am. I'm a gift; we are all gifts. It is up to me to tap into my gifts and share them with the world. In order to do that, I like to give myself some "me" time. I enjoy unwinding, reflecting, and stepping outside of my day-to-day norm. I also like to go to the Cheesecake Factory and have a passionfruit margarita. That always helps me. When you give to yourself, you have a clean soul, you can think clearly, and you're aware of your surroundings. By doing this, you allow the kindness of your heart to shine a light and give back to others.

> ***Betty Aquino*** *has devoted her career to positioning banking and legal services organizations, and the clients that they serve, for continued growth. She has created the strategies, teams, models, programs, networks, and products that have improved market positions, strengthened customer relationships, and elevated the financial performance of national law firm financing, commercial, and consumer lending platforms.*
>
> *In her current role as head of business development for Cartiga, she is building the capability to enable law firms and their clients to navigate challenges, seize opportunities, and optimize litigation outcomes. In less than six*

months, she secured ten million dollars in deals that have allowed litigation/contingency fee attorneys to secure access to capital.

She is an active member in her community, serving as a mentor to young professionals and providing financial literacy to elementary students in East Harlem. She is committed to empowering women in achieving career success. She developed the Women in Leadership Networking & Career Development Group to support women attorneys to solve problems and advance their careers. Betty earned a bachelor of science degree in accounting from Johnson & Wales University in Rhode Island.

TWO

GIVING SERVES YOUNG PEOPLE

Sylvia Brooks

God doesn't give you something hard to do unless it's for the benefit of someone else. These are the words of my husband, Errol. My husband was inspiring. I grew up in Houston's Third Ward, but my husband of almost forty years grew up totally different from me. He was from a very poor area in Honduras. The family moved to New York. They were very spiritual, and my husband had faith. I didn't have as much faith as he had, even though I thought I did. He helped me stop and listen to the messages around me, to what people were asking, to how I could be more helpful to people.

My husband knew everybody on our street. He would help people looking for jobs. He would often sit and talk with a neighbor who was ill. My husband and I have three sons, and when my sons were young, we had company all the time. The kids from the neighborhood were always running in and out of our home. It was a sacrifice. But when I look at where some of those young people are today, it is amazing. When my husband died in 2014, the people in the neighborhood missed him and appreciated what he did for them. My husband had kindness and gave the gift of his time. I had to learn that.

LEARNED GIVING

From my husband I learned how important it is for children to be taught very early how to give back. Giving back needs to start in kindergarten, or even before. My son, the director of athletics of Macalester College, is an advocate of my grandchildren giving back. My grandchildren who are four, ten, and fifteen are all doing some form of giving—to Girl Scouts, to their basketball group. Their church teaches giving too. Giving transcends home and school.

My grandson, who is four, did a Martin Luther King craft which he called "his project," and he made one for everybody. It is great to see him sharing so early.

I mentor the young leaders and young people coming behind me, including my nieces. I enjoy getting young people hooked up with the influential people I met while working for the United Way and Urban League. I try to get them in the right place and the right positions. One of my mentees from the Urban League who volunteered for the young leaders program is on City Council today, and one of them is running for mayor this year. I hired US Congresswoman Sheila Jackson Lee's daughter Erica to work as a tutor for the Urban League's youth leadership program called New Lights. The speaker could not be present at a program for the kids, so Erica—who was just a college student—spoke instead. She did a great job, and this beautiful, talented, smart young woman is now a senior staff member of the county commissioner. Young people are so talented, and it is fun to see them in positions where they are now giving back. For example, my niece and a couple of her friends chair the Conservancy of Emancipation Park in Houston.

UNITED WAY AND URBAN LEAGUE AS TRAINING GROUNDS

I came from the United Way as the director of planning and allocations. The Urban League was one of the United Way agencies. Serving the Houston-area Urban League was an honor but also a challenge. It was primarily a male-dominated leadership team, and I brought balance to the organization as a woman in leadership. I took the time to offer young women responsible positions. Some of the women may not have had the experience, but I knew they could do a particular job. My senior vice president was a woman. Of five people in leadership roles, three of them were women. It was important for other young women and the young children in our music program to see women lead. It was a joy.

When I was at the United Way in 1976, the leadership was primarily white and wealthy. I was from a totally different background. I was a civil rights baby; I came up during that time. I wasn't the first African American they hired, but I was one of few. I identified with the leadership and found people who supported me at the United Way. A large number of Jewish people on the board supported me. I knew that in order for me to make an impact there, I was going to have to take a lot and to give a lot. It was a difficult and challenging time, but I made sure my committees were balanced, integrated, and structured. I knew I was immature in terms of leadership, but I said, "I have got to do this not for me, but I must do this for the people coming behind me." It fuels me to see what I can do to benefit somebody else.

One of the programs that was dear to me was the one I set up for senior citizens who were in need of housing or home repair, or who were about to lose their homes. I was one of the people who set up the homeless coalition in Houston when I was at the United Way.

Houston was one of the original starters of Juneteenth. Texas created a state holiday. The Emancipation Park history project asked three people who were eighty years old about growing up in the Third Ward. I was one of them, and, for me, it was important to speak about the history of African American leadership. I've donated all of my papers to the library, because they may be helpful for future research. I have shared my history and all of the tools that I had to help people be the best they could be. My life has been devoted to that, and my life will end doing that. What you leave behind is important.

GIFTS TO SELF

At my age, I try to take care of myself better. I have a twin sister who lives three blocks away from me. I am kind to my sister. We have experienced loss; both of our husbands had cancer, so we are kinder and supportive of one another. We are both exercising (I love yoga) and eating better. Being an ongoing support to my sister is also a fitting deed.

> ***Sylvia K. Brooks*** *was the first female president and CEO of the Houston Area Urban League (HAUL) in 1990. Prior to her selection, she had served her community in many capacities: caseworker for child welfare services in Texas, professor in the Graduate School of Social Work at the University of Texas at Arlington, recruiter of minority women at the University of Massachusetts Dartmouth, and vice president of community problem-solving and fund distribution for the United Way of the Texas*

Gulf Coast. She received a bachelor of science degree in psychology from Texas Southern University in 1963 and would go on to receive a master of science degree in social work from the University of Southern California in 1969.

Under her administration, many new programs were instituted, including community outreach and program development. Reading skills programs, such as Watch Me Read, were offered at day care centers to help children develop literacy. In collaboration with IBM, computer training programs were instituted to enhance the skill set of those seeking employment. A new Business System Training Center was also opened as a resource that the community could use to train in the skills employers were seeking. Job fairs were held during Black History Month each February where five thousand people attended. Her most notable achievement was the Housing Counseling project that assisted and educated consumers on how to become homeowners.

In June 2007, after serving more than sixteen years as president and CEO of HAUL, she announced her retirement. Under her direction the agency volunteer staff grew to two hundred young professionals. She oversaw a forty-member *board and a $4.6 million annual budget. She currently lives in Houston's Third Ward and is a mother to three sons. She stays active within the community as a consultant to HAUL and within the organization she founded, the Third Ward Redevelopment Council.*

THREE

INSPIRING THE NEXT GENERATIONS OF GIVERS

Kian Brown

I grew up in Wilmington, North Carolina. My late father, Terry Brown, was a pastor. He was responsible for the prison ministry at our church. The prison ministry was about selflessness and the need to teach and train people who were in tough situations. From the prison ministry, I learned that when you tell people God loves them despite what they've done, you tell them there's still forgiveness, there's still redemption, and they are still a child of God. They can only think: you are right. My mom, Sherry Brown, was an educator. She spent most of her career working for the Department of Social Services in a receiving home for abused and infected children which was sponsored by

my hometown church. My mom was responsible for the children, and she stayed at the home with them. She would go grocery shopping, cook for them, and teach. Often, my mom would bring my sister and me with her to the home. The teenagers were from horrible situations. My sister and I saw, heard, and understood stories of pain and suffering. I once told my mom that she ruined us for good because we were taught how to always be generous, to give what we had, and to take care of people. This is why I do what I do.

I've been in situations I shouldn't have been in, and I should have been dead. I have had my testimony, but God has let me live. When you are blessed and you have a testimony, it's your responsibility to save others. That's what I think good deeds are. Doing good deeds is just who I am. I'm not a good guy all the time. I'm not bopping around on rainbows and sunshine, but my intentions are to serve people. My intentions are to be generous with my time, energy, resources, and whatever wealth I have. This is how I define philanthropic work.

Giving back makes me feel alive, and it reinforces that I matter. I teach that you matter, that you belong, and that there is something on the planet that won't get accomplished unless you do it. I teach, preach, scream, and holler this. When I give, it reinforces my own mattering, my calling, and the gifts God has given me.

Good deeds are important because they say: when in doubt, focus out. I focus out even when I'm hurting, tired, and sick. It hasn't always been easy, but my dad made it very clear to me that your calling always supersedes your comfort level, and even though you don't feel comfortable, that does not mean you are not called to do something. I'm driven by my Dad's message. I'm very sick with COVID right now, but the Bible says to be generous on every occasion (2 Corinthians 9:11). Giving when you're in doubt, messed up, hurt, and scared is like windshield wipers pushing aside your current situation so you may focus on somebody else.

MENTORING YOUNG PEOPLE IN COLLEGE

I specifically focus on student body presidents at historically Black colleges. I was student body president at North Carolina Central University (NCCU). When I was at NCCU, I wished someone had taken me under their wing or even given me a book to set me up to be a successful student leader. I was successful, but I did it on a solo tip and with God's grace. My legacy is NCCU. My Dad was the captain of the football team at NCCU in the 1980s, and I became Student Government Association (SGA) president in the 2000s. My cousin and my sister went to the school. So, the legacy of our family at NCUU is important. Recently, Proctor & Gamble did a documentary on the legacy of historically Black colleges and universities (HBCU) families, and they followed my family around NCCU; I appeared on national television delivering an inspiring narrative. The school is the biggest philanthropic work of my life. We aim to raise ten million dollars to name the School of Business after my father. I want to use my platform and my passion for my university to serve and be generous with my time and energy.

After college at NCCU, I moved to New York. I worked in New York for seventeen years. I was away from my family and the protection of an HBCU. As a North Carolinian country kid in New York, I had to learn on my own. I fell on my face and was lost.

Every day, I reached out to the current SGA president at my university. I also contacted other SGA presidents around the country, especially the SGA president of Bethune Cookman when they were protesting the college's president. Any time I see student leaders doing the work, I offer any advice or any support I can.

To train a student body president, I invited a student from North Carolina to visit me in New York for the summer. I took him to gatherings where he had to speak to strangers, write speeches, and do other things important to being an excellent student body president. I also took him to the gym, and we broke bread at church. He really listened and heard me. I didn't have all the answers. We didn't do everything I hoped that we would. But he is a now a law school student, and he sends me messages about what I taught him. Authentic moments with students who tell me years later that I challenged them make me want to continue to give back. The students learn how to have difficult conversations and how to apologize. I have a background in branding, marketing, and public relations, so I teach personal branding. I do a brand audit by opening a student's social media pages to see if their pictures match their descriptions of themselves. The exercise allows us to determine if there is a brand conflict. Students often tell me how much I have changed their lives.

I am committed to teaching young people emotional intelligence and social emotional learning. I have learned not coerce them to understand my vision or my dream for their lives, but to simply manifest the dream God gave me. I wrote a song called "Believe in Me," about one of my former students, a tall, Black, large skateboarder kid. On the outside, someone may think of him as a threat or menace, but he is a skateboarder signed to Pharell Williams's Ice Cream skateboard brand. The song says, "If you don't believe in yourself, believe in me."

I love mentorship because of the exchange. Sometimes, I feel the kids teach me far more that I could ever teach them. I give them content and subject matter, but I receive soft skills, love, and appreciation.

MENTORING YOUNG PEOPLE BY RETURNING TO AFRICA

I am passionate about West Africa and making sure young Black people have access to Africa.

In 2019, during "the year of return," I took sixteen teenage boys to Ghana. We raised money on our GoFundMe Page; some parents paid, and I used money my Dad left me. The teenagers were members of the Kappa League of the Montclair, New Jersey, alumni chapter of my fraternity, Kappa Alpha Psi.

In Africa, we put our feet in water where our ancestors were born, went through the door of no return, and served the community. I saw the kids grow, especially the president of the Kappa League. I saw how his leadership expanded; it was amazing.

I love Kumasi, Ghana. It is the heart of the Ashanti kingdom and where my ancestors are from. When I was there, I was told it was where I belonged. I can't remember anyone in my adult life telling me I belong somewhere. Maybe it is what they tell all Black Americans, but I didn't care. I began building in Kumasi and partnered with a nearby science and technology university. I want young people to study abroad and serve in Ghana. I also have another big goal: to take ten recently elected SGA presidents to Ghana for a two-week cultural immersion and leadership training. This will send them back on fire to their schools, having been seen, loved, heard, and supported. There's so much power in returning to your ancestral home.

GIFTS TO SELF

While mentoring youth and serving at NCCU, I also give to myself emotionally. I love taking care of myself, but I'm not good at it. I have to do better at understanding my capacity and being more powerful when I respond to someone with "not at this time." I love to meditate (following the work of Dr. Joe Dispenza), work out, and enjoy experiences such as Jazz at the Lincoln Center, going to the beach, and travelling. I enjoy a good cowboy ribeye, cabernet, and a little scotch.

> *Kian Brown is a passionate HBCU advocate, personal branding expert, and philanthropist who has earned the reputation as an ambassador of change and community leader in the greater New York City area and beyond. He is also widely known for his cutting-edge coaching strategy seminars that have empowered hundreds of people to date.*
>
> *Hailing from Wilmington, North Carolina, Kian studied at North Carolina Central*

University, where he proudly served as a student body president and senior vice president of the University of North Carolina Association of Student Governments. Right out of college, he continued to be drawn to positions of leadership and began to manage programs for Rush Communications. The CEO, Russell Simmons (also the cofounder of Def Jam Recordings) played an integral role in the beginning of his creative career, exposing him to prominent recording artists and industry moguls in the entertainment, media, and culture space.

Throughout the course of the next decade, Kian cultivated extensive expertise in elevating and expanding a multitude of reputable brands for public, private, and nonprofit sectors and everything in between. By 2012, he was a founding partner of the Millennium Sports Management Group, a nonprofit-centered management firm where he supports professional athletes and public figures.

In 2016, Kian Brown shifted his focus to the reality TV sphere and joined the cast of a digital series called #TheGraduatesNYC, showcasing his multifaceted life, from his journey as a media coach and speaker to bringing awareness to the importance of the preservation and elevation of historically Black colleges and universities.

Kian was part of the class of 2018 Most Influential People of African Descent Under 40 (MIPAD), in support of the International Decade for People of African Descent proclaimed by United Nations General Assembly Resolution 68/237. As a host and personality, Brown was featured in Century 21's "Adulting" campaign and has secured exclusive interviews with actors Willow and Jaden Smith, Clark Sisters heir Kierra Sheard, and most recently the president and first lady of Sierra Leone, as well as the grandson of Nelson Mandela, author Ndaba Mandela.

Kian Brown is a multifaceted professional on a mission to build brands, support the youth, and give back to his community. The spark of entrepreneurship and unwavering compassion have always served as his driving forces; he's in the class of 2018 Most Influential People of African Decent, part of the original cast of #TheGraduatesNYC on AspireTV, an advocate of positive change, personal branding expert, supporter of NYC youth, life-long philanthropist, and co-founder of The Maroon Society.

Editor's Note: In May of 2023, as we were preparing for publication, our friend, colleague, and contributing author Kian Brown transitioned without warning. In all areas of his life, Kian was known for practicing the art of good deeds. With Kian's family's blessings, we offer this contribution in his words, in his honor, as part of his well-respected legacy. Well done, Kian, well done.

FOUR

THE IMPACT OF GIVING *AND* *RECEIVING*

Bob Carter

Philanthropy has changed since I started decades ago because we now have data to study trends in philanthropy. In the past, we observed how people gave. We now have hard data on how people are giving and where they are giving. The only thing that hasn't changed is the human heart. The heart remains constant. It is always there, and it is always acting out. The basis of philanthropy is the human heart. I think a classic example of philanthropy and the heart is recently when Buffalo Bills football player Damar Hamlin suffered a cardiac arrest during a game against the Cincinnati Bangles. When he collapsed, the world forgot about the football game. America was pulling

for this young guy—a guy they probably never heard of prior to him collapsing. Some weeks before Damar Hamlin collapsed, he created a GoFundMe page to raise $2,500 to give toys to children for Christmas. After he collapsed, money started rolling in, and he raised over eight million dollars for toys. The human heart told everybody they had to do something to help the young man. People reacted the best way they could, which was to send money.

Philanthropy for me started in childhood. Growing up, I was taught to give to others. I learned from my father. He was my role model. Dad was generous in the community but not necessarily with finances. He was an active volunteer and a little league coach, and he did other volunteer work to make the community better. Dad taught me to never loan anybody money. Instead, give money because once you get into the loan business, you become a banker. If it doesn't harm your family, it is better to give money. I'm a lifelong Episcopalian and was taught to help the poor and to share wealth. Giving was part of my Christian upraising.

I worry about the state of young men today whenever I read a news headline stating that people were shot. I think: some young man lost his way, for whatever reason; he lost his identity and didn't know who he was, and this was his crazy and imbalanced way to gain recognition. To help young men, my wife and I give to projects that shape the lives of young men, and we have invested heavily into the Boys' Latin School in Baltimore—which my parents, who were only high-school graduates, worked very hard to send me to during the 1950s and 1960s. As a student at the Boys' Latin School, I learned that hard work pays off. I was graded each day, and I needed to be prepared. I was an all-state athlete in high school. I was taught how to appreciate the arts. I wrote poetry, and I loved literature. I wasn't one-dimensional, and I learned how to have a balanced life. The work habits that I developed at the Boys' Latin School from fourth grade to twelfth grade were a big part of my success. What the Boys' Latin School gave me makes me want to give back financially. I also wanted the school's value system to remain, so I became chairman of the board of trustees. I sent my sons to the school. When I was a kid and saw alumni of the Boys' Latin School giving back, I noticed that the givers were always smiling—how happy they were in giving. I always wanted to be a part of that. I've never seen a grumpy person giving a gift.

For the past fifteen years, I have worked with World Vision, the largest Christian charity in the world. I helped with World Vision's Vision Trips, and my wife and I did a Vision Trip to a mountain village in Honduras. It was a heartbreaking experience. We spoke with women from the village and asked them what they were most worried about. They were worried about their children, their future, and their health. Because of the water in the area, the hepatitis rate in the village was 90 percent. Early in the morning, the women were getting water from a dirty-bottomed residual rainwater pond. The villagers needed to connect a pipe to a lake that was higher up on the mountain to bring in clean water, but they didn't have the technology, tools, or resources to get the water. With the help of World Visions, we were able to bring clean water to most of the houses in the community, and local people were trained as plumbers to take care of the pipes. They learned how to keep the pipes clean and how to keep the water running. Within twelve months, hepatitis was in the past, and the crops also improved.

In my career in philanthropy, I have worked with celebrities, including amazing people like El Decker, the founder of Black & Decker, who humbly gave away millions to Johns Hopkins University. I have also watched unknown people quietly give away millions of dollars to help others. These were my role models.

Carlton Ketchum thought it was important for everyone to have access to good consulting. We were the first major consulting company to work with historically Black universities and colleges; we did not discriminate. Working in the African American community, I learned that the community fed their friends and their families. They sheltered them and gave them healthcare. They didn't have access to a lot, but they took care of others in their community in any way they could. From the Black community, I learned that if you're taking dinner to your next-door neighbor, you're a philanthropist. Philanthropy is not a monetary calculation. Philanthropic acts, like the ones I witnessed in Black communities, are just as vital and valuable. Statistically, we discovered that those who have less tend to give a larger proportion of what they have. There's room in philanthropy for everybody at every level to give.

PHILANTHROPY IS A RECIPROCAL ACT

On a bitter cold almost-Christmas day in Baltimore about ten years ago, I was walking to the Capital Grille to meet with some colleagues. I noticed a beggar sitting on the wall near the front door of the restaurant. I reached in my pocket and gave him a five-dollar bill. The man came rushing after me. When I saw the restaurant's doorman trying to protect the restaurant by pushing the smelly man out, I asked the doorman to let the man stay to get warm. I shook the man's hand, and he gave me a nylon bag with a set of fake pearl earrings in it. I thanked the man for the earrings and appreciated his generosity, but I resisted the earrings. He said I was generous to him, so he wanted to be generous to me. He insisted that I take the earrings, so I took them.

When I returned to my hotel that evening, I put the earrings in my briefcase. I met the man at the restaurant over ten years ago. I've had three briefcases since then, but I always remember to put the earrings in my briefcase. I travel with the earrings. They have been to the Middle

East and all over the world. The guy's generosity was a beautiful act of reciprocal philanthropy. The earrings reminded me that God is driving the reciprocal philanthropy that changes the world.

GIFTS TO SELF

Sometimes, I think the gift of giving is for me. When I am in the Starbucks line at the airport in the morning, I always buy for the person behind or in front of me, thinking maybe the person had a hard time getting there or struggled to buy their plane ticket. I buy them a cup of coffee and a couple of buns. Some people can't accept it. They think I have some angle. Those who do accept it appreciate it and tell me I started their day right. I get an enormous rush from hearing those words. I'm not Bill Gates, not the biggest philanthropist in the world, but I am grateful to be in a position where I can give.

That, and self-care is my reward. I'm a recovering alcoholic, and every day when I wake up, I thank God. My commitment for the day is to try to do the next right thing because I've been taught that a good life doesn't come instantly. It is a series of doing good things. When I started recovering from alcohol, I would treat myself to a weekly massage. I decided to make myself feel good about the change in my life, and the massages were a little payback for me.

At the end of almost every conversation, I say, "Take care of yourself." If you can't take care of you, then you can't take care of others. In closing, I am telling you to take care of yourself. If you feel sorry for yourself, go help somebody else and give them your time or money. I guarantee you'll feel better, and suddenly your problem won't be so big.

There is a philanthropist within you. If you notice a problem, you're the person who should do something about it. The great thing about philanthropy is the freedom to act on what you believe in and share your values with other people. Once you start doing that, you will discover that you pretty much share the same values as everyone else. You want a safe place for your family. You don't want people to go hungry.

You have a little bit of God in you. You were given the ability to know right from wrong and to make decisions. Most of the time, you know the right thing to do, and that is to help someone else.

Bob Carter is one of the world's most respected, experienced, and recognized experts in the areas of institutional strategy and philanthropy. During the past four decades, Bob has strengthened a variety of organizations throughout the world by helping them overcome challenges and capitalize on opportunities to be successful. Bob and his colleagues concentrate on building dynamic teams to deliver specific services that meet the unique needs of charities and donors. His service as a member and chair of numerous nonprofit boards lends firsthand experience to his governance counsel.

Bob established Bob Carter Companies in 2011 and currently serves as the chairman under the new Carter brand. Prior to forming Bob Carter Companies, Bob spent three years as a senior advisor for Changing Our World and Omnicom Nonprofit Group. Before this, he spent twenty-six years with Ketchum, one of America's largest fundraising consulting companies; in his last fifteen years with Ketchum, Bob was the president and CEO.

Bob is currently serving as a member of the Board of the World Health Organization (WHO) Foundation, Bridge Philanthropic Consulting, and the African American Development Officers (AADO) Network, where he is a founding board member. Bob is chair emeritus of the Association of Fundraising Professionals (AFP) International Board of Directors. Bob is also chair emeritus of the National Aquarium and is a current member and past chair of the Mote Marine Laboratory.

FIVE

PHILANTHROPY AND DOING GOOD DEEDS DURING A CRISIS

Rev. Jacques Andre DeGraff

Philanthropy should uplift. It ought to illuminate and heal. My mother personified this. She was a nurse. When I was in the sixth grade, I had a classmate who had her appendix removed. My mother was in charge of her recovery room, and she served as a comfort to my classmate. This was a way of life for my mother; she was always giving to others. As her oldest son, I followed in that tradition. She and my father, who worked for the Department of Defense, introduced me to a culture of philanthropy that goes beyond celebrity, people of achievement, or even corporate giving. It's what I like to call "kindness philanthropy."

Kindness philanthropy is when you get a bonus, put fifty dollars in a card, and give it to someone on a fixed income. It's when you give a student just starting college a handshake with something in it.

Character and authenticity need to match giving. Giving should be part of how we evaluate people. It should be a question we ask in courtships and in job interviews. We should be asked, "Who are you? How are you reflected beyond the material things you have acquired?" We have to challenge the acquisition of things as a measure of who we are and measure ourselves by how we impact others. Everybody has an obligation to give. It's mandated in the Bible, but it's also mandated by the American story. None of us got where we are by ourselves. Philanthropy ought to be what we do in our everyday life and be part of our culture.

As an advisor to the Nielson company, I followed consumer spending. Black folk in America spend $1.3 trillion a year on consumer goods. Five percent of that directed in an intentional philanthropic way could change our circumstances.

In the height of the 1960s, I was one of only two northerners to attend a precollege summer intensified training program at Morehouse and

Spelman college in Atlanta. I recall the Rolling Stones toured America with their hit song "I Can't Get No Satisfaction," and a fellow named James Brown was their opening act. On weekends, most students attending the precollege program went home or had family nearby they could visit. The English language arts instructor offered me and the other northerner an opportunity to visit her church. I was raised in an Episcopal church—also known as the frozen chosen—so as a kid from the Bronx, witnessing Baptist church worship was eye-opening. The music was amazing. The speaker one Sunday was Reverend Dr. Martin Luther King, Jr. My English language arts instructor didn't tell me that Dr. King—at the time the most famous Black man on the planet—was her brother. At the repast after the sermon and even while Dr. King was speaking, I could feel he was God's spokesperson. God was speaking through a man. When I was introduced to him, even as a teenager I realized that this was a moment that I would never forget. He had an aura. I left his presence mesmerized and inspired.

Years later, I thought I wanted to be an actor and was part of the National Black Theater. The National Black Theater required that you do three things: talk about falling or being in love, go to a Black bar, and go to a Black church. I'll skip the first two. I went to a Black church in Harlem on Father's Day, and I felt the same spirit that I had felt years before in Atlanta. I joined that church and stayed for fifty years. I became an ordained minister in that church. Along the way I found out the pastor of that church was Rev. Dr. Wyatt Tee Walker, Dr. King's chief of staff and the architect of the Birmingham freedom movement. As Dr. King's chief of staff, he was an advanced man of the movement and was hated by the Klan in the South. He would rarely appear in pictures with Dr. King because there were death threats on his life. He was put in prison, and yet he had this spirit. He worked with Harry Belafonte, organized events, dealt with donors, and was very good with money. He was the chair of the Freedom National Bank. He opened doors for me. I watched how he conducted and carried himself when an African immigrant by the name of Amadou Diallo was shot in the Bronx. We were on 161st Street trying to get to a prayer vigil that Rev. Sharpton conducted. There were snipers on the rooftops and helicopters flying through. The policed had cordoned off the area, and you couldn't just walk through. Rather than walking, Rev. Dr. Walker hopped over the barricade, and I had to hop over the barricade too. A policeman confronted Rev. Dr. Walker, and I had never seen a Black man confront a policeman the way he did. The policeman said, "You can't go here," and Rev. Dr. Walker said "Then arrest me." I could never imagine somebody challenging a policeman, and it was a Black policeman. Rev. Dr. Walker got right in his face and said, "Arrest me, but I'm going to that prayer vigil." The policeman was furious, but he was paralyzed by this act of bravery. It was a moment when Rev. Dr. Walker was standing on God's promise and standing on righteousness. If the policeman had hit him or arrested him, I made up my mind that he would have to arrest me too. I was the head of protocol and once executive director for the National Action Network. I went with Reverend Sharpton to meet with Castro and traveled with him to Sudan, so I've seen a lot. But that moment with Rev. Dr. Walker sticks out in my mind because it was inspirational. It was about the power of one: a made-up mind. I was the last person that Rev. Dr. Walker ordained. From that journey I learned my life's call is to serve and to give.

The notion of giving is central to who I am. Education and healthcare are two crisis issues that I focus on.

MOUNTAINTOP MOMENTS–MILLION MAN MARCH, EAGLE ACADEMY, CHOOSE HEALTHY LIFE

Giving is what I do. My mountaintop moments are those satisfying moments when the Almighty provides me with visions of how and what God wants me to give.

The time of the Million Man March was turbulent. Minister Farrakhan called the march, and the fact that he called it was controversial. Rev. Dr. Walker was not supporting it. Minister Farrakhan came to our church to meet with Rev. Dr. Walker and have a meeting with Black clergy. As God would have it, Rev. Dr. Walker couldn't make the meeting, so I hosted it. Something about the way Minister Farrakhan was organizing the march made me think we needed to go, but in our own way. Buses were leaving from New York City at midnight, which in my mind put them in Washington, DC at five o'clock or six o'clock for an eleven o'clock event.

I didn't think that made sense. Washington was terrified; they were on alert at the notion of a million Black men coming to Washington. The nation was hyperactive at the thought there was going to be violence. I got two buses and organized about one hundred men from across the city to come. Most of us dressed in black. Men from the choir of my church came. A Pulitzer Prize winner was in our group, as well as a commissioner from the Department of Mental Health and a family that ended up on the cover of *Time* magazine. One of the men in our bus is now the chancellor of the City of New York, and another is deputy mayor.

Instead of bussing to Washington, DC, where I knew it would be a problem, we went to Silver Springs and took the commuter train to Washington. Black women, out of respect, could not go to the mall, but they wanted to see a million Black men, so we went through an arch of sisters who wore African attire. I told each of the men in my group to line up behind me and put their right hand on the right shoulder of the man in front of them. When we got to the mall, a million Black men were already there. It was a biblical moment. Some of the most famous men in America were on the platform.

When we left, sisters came and gave each of us a rose and some fried chicken. On the bus ride home, each man got up and testified. I played the movie *Glory*. As the final scene in the movie approached, I cut it off. Everybody was furious. I responded: "They all died on that day, but on this day we're gonna pick up the blood-stained banner and hold it high for them!" When we came off that bus, the *New York Times* took a picture of my men and ran a story on us. It was one of the most satisfying moments in my life of service.

When we came back from the Million Man March, we were inspired, and we wanted to do something that would leave a legacy that would live beyond our lifespan, so we created the Eagle Academy. One of its first principals is now the chancellor of the New York City school system. I have five grandsons, and the fifth grandson graduated from the Eagle Academy. During the intake process, a man approached the principal while I was there. The man and his son lived in Far Rockaway, a long way from the school, which was in the Bronx. The son had to take two trains to get to the school. They were homeless, and the father asked, "Would you take my son because I want my son to be an eagle?" The moment imbued in me the mission that not only do we have to give, but we also have to model. I am the one who gave the school its name. When people asked, "Why don't you call it the Colin Powell school?" I responded that we need a *new* Black man. We have Black men standing on corners with their drawers showing—Black men who speak disrespectfully to Black women. We need a new Black man. We need Black men who are eagles, and that argument won. We promote, inspire, and motivate eagles. The eagle doesn't fly in a flock. We need men who don't want to be like the crowd. We need men who can stand on their own. The school started in the Bronx, but there are now six schools. The schools are all in the toughest zip codes in the city, and there is one in Newark. At times, it is very challenging. We lose young men to the streets. Every year somebody gets shot, commits suicide, or something else terrible happens. It is gut wrenching, but it underscores the importance of the work that we have to do.

I am the minister for the twenty ministers—including Raphael Warnock, our clergy for Atlanta—of the twenty churches involved in the national initiative Choose Healthy Life, which started around COVID in Black churches in Newark, New York, Detroit, DC, and Atlanta.

We have full-time health navigators who deal with vaccinations and testing; we sponsor Wellness Wednesdays, receive funding from Quest Diagnostics, and have the United Way as a partner.

The pandemic crisis played a role in me giving back. I am the chair of the Friends of Harlem Hospital. For weeks, people were working double shifts and taking off their clothes outside their front doors when they came home because they didn't want to kill their family with a virus they brought home. On Mother's Day, I organized for the women in the intensive care unit and emergency room a soul food meal from Melba's Restaurant in Harlem. We had African drummers, and the local fire department blasted their horns outside to salute the women. We had a dozen roses sent to the executive director of the hospital. I also made a video. I like to think we offered comfort to the hospital staff by outlining our appreciation. We showed them they were in our prayers. I trusted God for the ministry of presence. It's important to write a check, but it is not enough. It is important to serve.

During the pandemic, we were advised to not to go in the hospital. I had what was equivalent to a VIP pass, so I would go there. There were times I visited and knew that would be the last time that person would see anybody, and it would be the last time that I would see them. It was a rough time to serve. Statues and plagues from the Civil War a hundred fifty years ago still stand. More people died in the pandemic than the Civil War. We have scars and post-traumatic stress from the pandemic. Suicides are up, violence is up, reading scores for our students have plunged, weddings were canceled, and life expectancy has plunged. Some churches were closed for two years, and some went out of business. We're dealing with a silent storm. Part of my ministry is to speak to that storm. Everyone is carrying what I like to call a secret sorrow.

GIFTS TO SELF

In addition to giving, I have also faced a personal crisis. About twenty years ago, I was unemployed and struggling with drugs. Two men from my church took me to a rehab facility; they never said a word of condemnation or judgment, and I found my way back.

My wife of forty-eight years was the person who called the two men. She has been a blessing. I don't want her to ever think I take her for granted. She's put up with me for so long. She's the best thing that ever happened to me. She has been my partner in this enterprise of my ministry. Every day she makes a difference.

Helping others requires a discipline of work life balance. Ministers in particular—type-A personality men and women—can lose balance. When you lose balance, you may not be aware that the needle is pointed to empty until something happens.

I was hospitalized with diverticulitis. When they diagnosed me, I realized my contributions to my circumstance: I was burned out, and to address my burnout, I had binged on pistachios, walnuts, and Hershey's Kisses, which took a toll on my digestive system. The binging was an escape from what was burning me out: that my daughter died by her own hand. I went to California for her remains, and I preached at her funeral, but I was burned out inside. At the same time, the best man at my wedding was dying. He died six months after my daughter's funeral. After both their deaths, I couldn't get out of bed. I've had to learn that some days, I have to let whatever happens that day happen without me, so I can stay on the battlefield.

*In a room full of dignitaries and media mavens, **Rev. Jacques DeGraff** stands out. His calm and engaging demeanor draws you in, forcing you to listen and understand his points of view on current issues. In a disarming manner, he uses his sharp wit and command of information to dispel the opposition's case without being dismissive. In fact, he loves a rigorous debate and, armed with a lifetime of implausible experiences that he weaves into his presentation, he usually wins the argument. Invariably, these wins are on behalf of the disenfranchised. For most of his life, Rev. DeGraff has been an outspoken advocate for economic and social justice for people of color. Currently, Rev. DeGraff is an active member of the One Hundred Black Men of New York, past vice president, and a member of the founding chapter of the international organization. The One Hundred Black Men of New York is a philanthropic organization dedicated to educating and empowering African American youth. Rev. DeGraff and his One Hundred Black Men brethren founded the Eagle Academy Schools for young boys throughout New York City.*

SIX

SERVICE WITHOUT JUDGMENT

Latoya Henry

I don't want to give for the purpose of feeling good; I want to give for the purpose of giving, to give purely without wanting an accolade, affirmation, or a pat on the back.

The earthquake in Haiti was a turning point for me. I thought of how an earthquake could have impacted St. Lucia. My grandmother, who was a teacher, and my grandfather gave me the opportunity to be here in the states, to live a life far different from the one I would have lived if I was still in St. Lucia. I did fundraisers for Haiti to raise awareness as well as funds. My friends and I created a campaign to identify what was going on and how it impacted the people there.

I supported other friends who did focus events. I helped raise money for Habitat For Humanity.

I give to my alumnae association, the New York Alumnae Association of Spelman College, and to my church, First Corinthian Baptist Church (FCBCNYC), but I realized giving is not only monetary. I love the philanthropic space so much! I hosted fundraising events, including cocktail parties.

GIVING IS GOOD DEEDS WITHOUT JUDGMENT

Through service, I have learned that anyone can be in anyone's shoes. At Usher's New Look (UNL) Foundation, where I oversee all the programs, we took young people to a food bank in northern California. Usher's vision is to provide young people ages fourteen to twenty-four with access, opportunity, and resources. We call our young people "disruptive innovators," and we focus on four pillars: talent, education, career, and service. We have a strong financial literacy component and afterschool trainings on branding, leadership, and networking. We want young people to have an impact on the world. We host events that activate their voices and lend support they need to be change agents because it's essential that youth spark positive change in the world.

At the food bank, we discovered that those who came there for supplemental food were making on average $125 thousand a year. That a person could make six figures and still need to go to the food bank demonstrated that anybody can be in that position. It gave me an added level of empathy. A person who has a ten-thousand-dollar handbag has equal value to the person living on the street. Just by being here we all have value; we're all a gift to the world.

It feels good to give, to do good deeds for another person without judgment.

Good deeds are teeny-tiny decisions. If someone is crying or looking distressed, and you ask how they are feeling—that is a good deed. I incorporate good deeds into my daily life. For example, I had leftover food from a party at my house and gave it to a gentleman that I saw on the street, and I saw him carry the tray of food to others nearby. I consult pro bono for nonprofits and send toys to my friend's sorority.

GIFTS TO SELF

I spent time at ISKCON, a temple in Berkeley, California. That experience taught me how to see the spirit and soul within everyone and to love myself through acceptance of the good, the bad, and the ugly. That is the baseline of how people love themselves. I love myself by accepting everything that I have control over and everything that I don't have control over. At the temple, I learned that service is my true calling. My background is in public relations marketing and events, so while I was at the temple, I created an e-mail campaign and a website, wrote fundraising letters, developed a communications plan, and created fundraising event.

I love myself internally by pouring in and nurturing. I make an effort every day to read something that helps me work on myself, for example, Iyanla Vanzant's *Until Today!* as well as books on gratitude, or I listen to a sermon.

Luxuriating at a wellness retreat is an act of self-love, for me. A little bit of luxury outside helps with the love inside.

Latoya Henry *is a marketing, public relations, and events executive with more than* *fifteen years experience in the corporate and nonprofit sectors. But it's her experience as a high school teacher that has inspired and invigorated her to lend her expertise to children and education-focused nonprofits like SFK— Success for Kids, A Better Chance, Children of Promise, and Usher's New Look; to planning Young Leadership functions and award/fund-raising ceremonies; and to managing community relationships. She has mastered the fine art of raising funds and awareness with panache through provocative, experiential events.*

Her current role as vice president of programs and partnerships at Usher's New Look allows her to ignite the spark in young people. Through this role, she's able to help them realize their gifts and talents and show them how they can share those gifts with the world through their education, career, and service to improve their lives and the lives of those in their communities. She is responsible for creating enrichment experiences, identifying and collaborating with strategic partners, and increasing awareness of the work that UNL does nationwide.

SEVEN

FAITH-ANCHORED GIVING

Jarred Howard

When we do good things, it pleases God. For those of us who believe in God and have a relationship with God, we recognize that good things are God things. The word "good" is derived from the word "God."

My faith and my relationship with the Almighty compels me to give. That is my motivation. It is my devotion to, affection for, and acquiescence to God that fuels me to give back. I hope what people experience from my giving is a deep affection from God.

Giving is a general principle by which I govern my life. When I give back, I'm living in my purpose. Doing good deeds helps me affirm to myself that I'm living in

my purpose and with intent. When I was in college, there was a guy who was a paraplegic. Often as I navigated the college campus, I was compelled to push his wheelchair. Helping the guy in the wheelchair encouraged my spirit. It wasn't always convenient to help him, but when he needed me, I made myself available for him, and it buoyed my commitment to doing good deeds.

There's never been a time in my life where I haven't been on the receiving end of other people's benevolence or grace. When I was younger, my aunts and uncles collected money for me to get a video game system because my mom wasn't able to buy me one. Many of my cousins came from two-parent households; they were going to enjoy the new video games, and my aunts and uncles didn't want me to feel left out. My upbringing was rocked with people who have given to me from the very beginning.

I make it a general principle to be courteous and accommodating when possible. When I'm driving, I am aware that I'm not the only driver on the highway. Other people have places to go and people to see. They have things to do as much as I do, so I try to allow people to get on the highway and not be selfish. It's one of the ways and in my daily life that I give.

I'm a giver. I don't consider myself to be rich. I've given thousands of dollars to charities annually. My wife and I are big benefactors of Saint Jude Children's Hospital, our local church, and many other churches that have missions that align with who we are. We are major givers to various ministry efforts such as Our Daily Bread, and we give to the United Way. My wife and I don't dictate where our kids give. We want them to make their own decisions in that regard, but we do want them to be givers.

I've got a couple of degrees, both of which are in business. The foundation courses were micro- and macroeconomics. Understanding how economics work compels me to give. Without investment, you won't realize a return. This is the biblical principle of seed (some investment) and harvest (return). Understanding the nuances of economic development, specifically economic development in underserved communities, through a biblical lens has helped me be a more intentional giver.

GIFTS TO SELF

I forever eat from the table of the elderly. The foundation of my affinity for doing good comes from my upbringing, from the way I was raised. My mother and my grandparents taught me that good deeds must be part of the experience when people encounter you. My grandfather was sixty years my senior, and he fed me—I don't mean just physical food—in a way that still produces results today. I make mentoring a matter of principle because of him. I've discovered that I can feed myself by feeding others.

Jarred Howard is principal of Sable Brands, LLC, and chief executive officer at the National Juneteenth Museum.

A Fort Worth native, Jarred holds a bachelor of business administration degree from the University of North Texas and a master of business administration degree from Dallas Baptist University. Jarred launched his career in JPMorgan Chase's consumer banking division and later led marketing teams at Daimler-Chrysler Financial Services. In 2006, Jarred commenced a twelve-year stay at BNSF Railway, where he led a team in the consumer products business unit before assuming leader-ship of their economic development division. In 2018, Jarred became a department head at the Fort Worth Chamber of Commerce, and in 2020, he was recruited to lead Bell Textron's external affairs division.

Jarred's hobbies include visiting African countries and studying the residual impact of the African diaspora.

EIGHT

GIVING IS LOVE IN ACTION

Max and Lillie Larsen

MAX

My wife Lillie and I always find a way give to each other and to others. We both grew up in Kansas and lived in small towns that were about fourteen miles apart. We started dating in high school and went to separate colleges, but we saw each other during the summer. I'm a year older than Lillie, so after I graduated from college, I went to the University of Kansas with her for grad school, and we got married there.

For Lillie and me, the art of giving is not passive. Most of our giving is with organizations which allow us to play an active role on

the board of directors and to assist with getting things done. We give in monetary ways, but most importantly, we give our time. We are involved in our community. For ten years, we worked with the Meadowlark Festival and sponsored a high school contest for Nebraska students who played string instruments. The students were awarded prizes and an opportunity to perform at a concert. We also contributed to the growth of the University of Nebraska–Lincoln Theatre Department by holding social events to increase and boost ticket purchases. At our church, the Westminster Presbyterian Church in Lincoln Nebraska, I served as an elder and session. Lillie was a deacon. For twelve years, I was vice president and president of the Nebraska State Board of Education; it was because of Lillie's encouragement to run that I won. I served on the Lincoln Symphony Orchestra with Lillie's help in fundraising for the orchestra. We auctioned a baton, and the highest bidder was given the opportunity to conduct the orchestra. I won the baton, but I was afraid to conduct, so Lillie stepped in for me and was the highlight of the show. I served on the board of the public service law firm Nebraska Appleseed, where a young woman was executive director working to increase the minimum wage in Nebraska. She needed $2,500 to hire people to get extra signatures. After a talk with Lillie about this opportunity to make a difference in the lives of poor people in Nebraska, I donated the money, so no one would have to work three jobs just to get by. With Lillie at my side, I had the guts to step up and help.

Lillie served on the board of the Lincoln Symphony and was president of the Lincoln Symphony Guild and president of the Friends of LSG, where she raised money to build a performing arts center. She volunteered with the Lincoln public schools, served as the president of the Lincoln School Board, and was the vice president of the Nebraska State Board of Education. For over twelve years, she has served the Lincoln East Rotary Club as Scholarship Chair, where she oversees the program and evaluates the applications for the four scholarships awarded to graduating high school seniors who live in Nebraska and stay to attend college. The students so appreciate the scholarship.

Lillie and I believe it is important to incorporate goods deeds into our daily life—tipping waiters well and telling their bosses they did well, for example, especially as we have done a lot of international travelling. We've visited sixty different countries. People don't get enough praise. Often when somebody passes away, I call the spouse and talk to them for a few minutes.

I am mindful of how I give to people. How you deliver a message has such a big impact, so I never tell people that's absolutely the wrong way to do something. I tell them there's another way to do it or have you thought about doing it this way. It helps them to find a better way without feeling bad about themselves. Yes, I want to tell people how to lead their lives, but I've learned that's not a good idea. It is more helpful for me to understand how they are leading their lives, offer suggestions, and help them to reach success. That's giving.

LILLIE

My dad was a dentist, and the work of my father showed me how to help other people. We went to church every Sunday, and he would meet us after church. One Sunday I asked Mama, "Why does Daddy go to the office every Sunday?" and she answered, "He goes to the office to take care of people who can't afford dental care." The message I received from my father's acts of goodness was to always help other people.

Giving back is like a circle. It always finds its way back to you. The generous work of my father lives on in our son Charlie, who is a pediatric dentist. He operates on children with cleft palates, but like his grandpa he doesn't charge the parents who can't afford it. Charlie told me that he got through a major surgery by dreaming his grandpa was standing beside him.

Max has always been devoted to helping people. I learned this when we were travelling on a train from Philadelphia to New York. A woman with a baby was loaded down with all of her belongings. Max jumped up like Superman and helped her up the steps with the baby. She dropped her purse, and Max asked the conductor to retrieve it from the tracks. The woman bent down to the ground and wrapped her hands around Max's legs to say thank you. I later learned from Max that she was an abused woman who was running away.

I was a high school teacher and have a master's degree in education, but after our sons were born, I stopped teaching and dedicated my time to my family. For twenty-five years, Max commuted weekly to Washington, DC, and came home on the weekends. When he retired, he went to DC for ten more years. I stayed home and took care of the household. In Washington, Max was responsible for a lot, but he called nightly to review our day and help our sons with their homework. He was always devoted and committed to our family. Max doesn't think of supporting our family as a good deed, but I think supporting our family is a good deed.

It takes so little to do a good deed. When I am making an appointment with the doctor and someone picks up the phone, I thank them at the end of the conversation. I call and speak with my ninety-four-year-old brother weekly. I have lost too many people in the last five years, so I call people regularly. Each time I call my sister-in-law who is ninety-one, she says, "Thank you. I needed the call." I don't think calling is doing something tremendous, but I am a firm believer that most of the problems in the world today are about communication. The best way to keep a family unit close is to communicate.

GIFTS TO SELF

Lillie: Max and I practice self-care. I walk with Max each morning. But I also think self-care is the relationship we have with each other and our friends. We stay positive because of relationships. Every Friday evening at five o'clock, we get together for a couple of hours with a group of friends to have cheese and crackers. I also like parties. For our sixtieth anniversary, we had a big party for one hundred people.

Every night before we go to bed Max and I say, "I love you." We also ask each other, "What you are doing tomorrow, and how can I help you accomplish that?" I am always happy to help Max and our family. We are a close-knit family. When Max retired, I asked that we build a house big enough for all our kids and grandkids. We have eight bathrooms; everyone has a bedroom, and the house is always available for when the family wants to come and stay with us.

For the past sixty years, Max and I have given to each other, to our family, and to the world. Max has been my teacher. I have learned from him what happiness is: to do the important things to help family and other people.

Max: Every morning when we wake up and every night when we go to bed, Lilli and I say, "I love you." We also leave notes for each other. In the summertime, I leave a note for her when I'm working in the garden because

I don't want her to worry if she comes home and doesn't find me. When Lillie goes out, she leaves a note for me. I care for Lillie by listening to her. I never isolate her, and I include her in everything. Before COVID, I was going to the gym every day. Because of the COVID shutdown, Lillie and I started walking around the lake in the back of our house every day after we ate breakfast.

If someone would ask me when a simple kind word impacted my life in a big way, I would say it was when Lillie said "yes." That has led Lillie and me to celebrate sixty years of marriage. Lillie's "yes "has led to our three sons: Michael, professor of statistics; Paul, associate counsel at PHRMA; and Charlie, director of pediatric dentistry at Stony Brook Dental School. And Lillie's "yes" has led to six lovely grandchildren. I hope my grandkids will remember the love Lillie and I put into action.

Lillie Larsen is a mother, former school-teacher, and wife devoted to the betterment of the world around her. Always taking an active role in her community, Lillie served on the Board of the Lincoln Symphony for many years and served as president of the Lincoln

Symphony Guild. In addition to her volunteer work, Lillie is an avid fundraiser for charities near her heart—raising $300 thousand for a performing arts center during her time as president of Friends of Lied.

Graduating from Paola High School in 1959, Lillie was active in the Thespian Society and editor of the Paola High student newspaper before attending the University of Kansas. After graduating in 1963 with her degree in French and secondary education, Lillie taught at DeSoto High School. After moving to Lincoln in 1966, Lillie received a fellowship at the University of Nebraska to study how elementary education and social work could improve learning. She was awarded a master's degree in elementary education from University of Nebraska–Lincoln and took additional courses in gifted education which led to her observing schools across Nebraska.

After Lillie's sons—Mike, Paul, and Charlie—were born, Lillie decided to take a break from her career and devote herself to her family. However, her ambitious spirit couldn't deny her teaching roots which led Lillie to volunteer in Lincoln Public Schools (LPS) where she was elected and re-elected to the Lincoln

---

School Board for twelve years, serving as president for one year. After retiring from the LPS School Board, she served one term elected to the Nebraska State Board of Education, serving as vice president for two years.

Dr. Max Larsen *began his career in academia as a professor of mathematics and then as dean of the College of Arts and Sciences at the University of Nebraska, where he focused on increasing external funding for research, development, and performance. As an academic leader, he emphasized excellence and measurability of results and impact to strengthen the college's fundraising efforts.*

Dr. Larsen worked for the Gallup Organization as managing partner for twenty-five years, managing large-scale consulting and research projects for government agencies, health organizations, and financial institutions. Larsen has the experience and educational background necessary to manage complex, large-scale engagements and to advise organizations on how to measure and improve performance.

His career as managing partner for government services for the Gallup Organization included strategic planning for business development and operational improvements while founding and growing Gallup's work with federal agencies. As a manager, Larsen was an enthusiastic developer of talent for Gallup and in Gallup's client organizations. As a contractor for federal agencies, he often established measurement systems to support strategic planning and to monitor success in implementation. Data from employees, customers, and operational outcomes were used to sustain changes. His role was frequently to train agency leaders to implement effective policies to improve performance and to provide measurement systems to sustain improvement efforts.

Upon retirement he formed a small company focusing on helping agencies and individuals improve performance through executive coaching and consulting. More recently he joined the consulting company Bridge Philanthropic Consulting LLC to provide strategic institutional capacity building to improve performance.

NINE

DISCOVERING YOURSELF THROUGH GOOD DEEDS

Reggie Van Lee

People often ask me, "What should I do to become more philanthropic?" My strategy was to recognize what am I passionate about. Then I decided what I can give. I tell people to find an organization they are passionate about; not the hot project that everyone else is claiming, but an opportunity for their involvement to be genuine. Identify what you love and make that your platform for giving.

Doing good deeds and being a person of service came from my parents. Even after their deaths, I harken back to the things they told me. I learned we are here on this earth to be a service to each other. My parents were not wealthy, but they were givers. In large and

small ways, they gave. After thirty-two years at the management consulting firm Booz Allen Hamilton, I retired in 2016. When I was at Booz, I was one of two Black partners. I was in meetings talking about things that I didn't want to talk about, going to dinners that I didn't want to go to, eating food I didn't want to eat, and playing golf when I didn't want to play golf. I complained to my parents about how lonely it was. My father told me, "It may be lonely at the top, but it is crowded at the bottom. You don't like crowds," he said, "so instead of cursing the fact that you are in a room by yourself, bring other people in the room." My father helped me crystallize my legacy. I've discovered that my legacy is about getting into a room that I'm not supposed to be in and bringing other people in the room who are not supposed to be there. I am committed to opening doors, providing a glide path, and seeing someone thrive and flourish in a space they deserve to be in when someone thought they shouldn't.

I am convinced that whatever I put out into the universe comes back to me threefold, both good and bad. So, I am always trying to do good because I want that good to come back to me. In honor of my older sister, I established a scholarship for undergraduate performing arts students at Howard University. On the television program *Pose*, there is a character called Damon that I really like. He is a dancer who was kicked out of his house by his family when they find out he is gay. He was homeless and moved to New York and slept in the park. The summer after the first season of *Pose*, I saw the man who played Damon at an event at Lincoln Center. He came up to me and said, "I am Ryan Swain, and I went to Howard on your dance scholarship." I had no idea I had anything to do with the phenomenal character I watched on television.

One day, I was having dinner at a restaurant in New York with about eight friends. When we finished eating our meals, the lovely young waitress said she wanted to treat us to dessert. She said she wanted to treat us because she went to Howard and received my scholarship. She also told me that she called three of her classmates who also received my scholarship, and they wanted to come to the restaurant to meet me.

I didn't go bankrupt supporting the scholarship program at Howard, but it has made such a huge difference. I don't know the students who receive the scholarship at Howard, but the students know who I am. Often they come up to me and say, "You don't know me, Mr. Van Lee, but I received your scholarship at Howard, and that changed my life." Educational philanthropy has allowed me to understand more about the real needs people have in the world and how I can be helpful. When I give, so many surprises come to me.

I have learned that every interaction with a person is an opportunity to build a relationship. When I lived in Washington, DC, a homeless man sat near the 7-Eleven where I would often go for delicious donuts. I frequently gave the man ten or twenty dollars. One night when it was raining, I gave him fifty dollars and my umbrella when I left the store. Several months later, I ran into the man on the street, and he told me he had a job. He thanked me for my kindness and for treating him like a real person. A small deed turned out to be a big one. I was able to build the homeless man's confidence and respect him as a good and worthy person.

I was one of the founding donors for the National Museum of African American History and Culture. I hosted an event at my house, and I convinced four wealthy friends, together with myself, to be founding donors. I'm proud to say that I never took help for granted. Community has always meant something to me. Growing up, I went to an all-Black church, and I lived in an all-Black neighborhood in Houston. I have hosted a friends and family day for my church at my house, which is a compound I built for my family in Houston that sits on land my great-grandmother purchased in 1899. I cherish my church members. Being a Black gay kid, I have never felt judged by the community, and I was comfortable with being myself. When I went to MIT, the church prayed for me. They would send me an envelope with a five-dollar bill wrapped in a Kleenex. How could I not want to do something for people who did something for me at a time when I couldn't do anything?

Large and small gifts have been given to me that inspired and motivated me to pass on a blessing. When I went to college, all of my four older sisters had graduated from college and were working. Each of my sisters gave me a credit card. I had a Lord & Taylor's, Saks Fifth Avenue, Brooks Brothers, and Visa card. I could spend two hundred dollars per month per card. My sisters did an amazing philanthropic deed that helped me get through school with a good self-image.

I recall my mother saying, "Never put a period where God has put a comma." I worked for Booz for two years so my student loan to Harvard's business school was forgiven. I planned to work for Booz for two years and stayed for thirty-two years. If I hadn't gone to Booz, I would not have had this great career. I would not have gone to business school. I did two or three things in my life that led to something magnificent, and those things led to more that was magnificent.

GIFTS TO SELF

People approach life with fear of the next life and the unknown. I am excited about the unknown. Every time I have stepped into something new, I couldn't have imagined what happened. There are so many moments where I never know who I may meet, and I am surprised at how much of an impact my good deeds have made. For me there is nothing like the feeling that I get when someone walks up to me and tells me that my actions have changed their life.

Reggie Van Lee is the chief transformation officer at the Carlyle Group, helping ensure that the firm is maximizing its market competitiveness and operating most effectively and efficiently as an institution. From his thirty-two years at Booz Allen Hamilton—where, before he retired as executive vice president, he led numerous businesses, including the US Telecommunications Practice, the US Computers and Electronics Practice, the global Media & Entertainment Practice, the US Federal Health Practice, and the Commercial Solutions business— Reggie brings decades of experience driving growth and best-in-class performance. At Carlyle, he leads the development of new and innovative ways to enhance the firm's business processes, drive faster decision making, and contribute to continued profitable growth. Prior to Booz Allen, he served as a research engineer with Exxon's production research company. Reggie is a member of the board of directors of Fortitude Re, ProKarma, Gallup Inc, the Women's Venture Capital Fund II Advisory Board, Washington Performing Arts, National CARES Mentoring Movement, John F. Kennedy Center for the Performing

Arts, Washington Nationals Philanthropies, Studio Museum in Harlem, the Public Theater, and the Juilliard School. He formerly sat on the boards of the Evidence Dance Company, the Dance Theatre of Harlem, and the Washington Ballet. He was named one of the top twenty-five consultants in the world by Consulting magazine, selected as a Washington Minority Business Leader by the Washington Business Journal, and named Black Engineer of the Year by Black Engineer magazine. He holds both a bachelor of science and a master of science in civil engineering from MIT and an MBA from Harvard University.

TEN

THE PRIVILEGE OF GIVING BACK AND MENTORING

Rustin M. Lewis

"To whom much is given, much is expected" is a quote from the Bible that comes to my mind when I think of how fortunate I am. The word *privilege* is a such a bad word nowadays. I've had them, but I take those privileges and invest them in somebody else. When you have opportunities, you can be selfish, but privilege means you have to do some retrospective and introspective thinking. You have to think, "How can I give more and not take, take, take?" By helping others, you become more thankful for what you have. You have a better perspective on life.

Empathy and kindness are two philanthropic traditions that I hope to pass along to my daughter. Empathy

is critical. You have to understand that not everyone has the same situation. We need to be empathetic to everyone with a willful intention to understand that we are all in this together, and not look at the world solely through our own lens. Whether you're in Jamaica or Egypt, we're all on this planet together. Do your part; the village is on fire. That is my message about mentoring.

I moved to Washington, DC, to work for an organization called College Bound. While working for that organization, I met a young man who was probably in the tenth grade. The young man lived on the backside of the Capitol, which is about five miles from the Capitol, yet he did not know what the Capitol was. That was an indictment of our community. He was born and raised in Washington, DC, and five miles beyond his community was the Capitol, but he was not given exposure beyond his community. The Capitol, the monuments that people across the world know about, might as well have been across the world for him. He inspired me. When I took the job with College Bound, I wanted to run a nonprofit. I was excited about the mission of the organization, which was preparing kids for college, but it was meeting that young man that laser focused me on the need for mentorship in order to see beyond their community walls.

Running College Bound, I was able to help 150 kids a year complete middle school and high school, and get accepted to college. That was my purpose and my passion. A young man in the program had a slight learning disability. In the College Bound program, he completed high school with honors, was given a scholarship, and attended a HBCU. Years later, I was preparing to run for City Council, and I ran into him in the grocery story. He volunteered to help me with my campaign. He knocked on doors and did anything that my campaign needed. Then he posted on social media his appreciation for allowing him to help me! He shared how much he respected me. His help with my campaign was one of the greatest feelings I have experienced in my life. I've mentored two other young men in DC—helped them to identify jobs and get into college, and motivated them to stay on the right path after they were released from the juvenile justice system.

When I moved on to other nonprofits, I found other means of creating vehicles for mentorship, for example the National Cares

Mentoring Movement in Atlanta. I had the pleasure of working with Tommy Dorch, who was the chairman of the board, and the founder, Ms. Susan L. Taylor. We set up opportunities to mentor young people around the country, particularly persons of color. It was a machine that constantly churned to help recruit people of color to help other people. We would ask three or four people to get together and commit to working with one youth. Each mentor would share time with the youth; the youth would get three mentors.

You don't have to sign up for a mentoring program to mentor someone. I see it all the time in the neighborhood barbershop. A young man will sit in the barber's chair, and the barber will say, "Hey man you need to leave those boys in the street alone" or "Pull up your pants."

The One Hundred Black Men of America's motto is, "What they see is what they'll be." I worked for the organization and watched members inspire the next generation through example. Having a role model you can look up to gives the youth an opportunity to have experiences that broaden their horizons.

DONATING

One thing that bothers me is the misconception that people of color, particularly African Americans, don't donate, that we don't give back. A recent report by the Kellogg Foundation says collectively African Americans gave eleven billion dollars in a single year. Think about all the lives we impact through our gifts.

A lot of what the Black community gives is focused on commitment to religion and education. Those are probably the most significant funding areas.

When my first wife passed away in 2005, I established a scholarship in her memory for students who completed the College Bound program. I donate money to organizations where I've served on boards: the East River Family Strengthening Collaborative, the Owen McCauley Dance Company, and the HD Woodson Stem Academy, which is an organization that helps young people develop technology and coding skills.

Just like breathing, mentoring and giving need to be part of us—something that we do. Small deeds are large deeds. For example, if you help someone get out of the juvenile justice system and get a job, it becomes a large deed because you have influenced their family for generations.

GIFTS TO SELF

I did not have children until fifteen months ago. For fifty-one years, I could be *me* focused. Lately, I'm doing more soul searching and realizing kindness is powerful because it evokes action. We can all do better at being kind, myself included.

Every single one of us will leave this earth, and we'll leave a footprint. The question is: What is the footprint? I want my family and my community to say, "Rustin's footprint is an entire life dedicated to mentorship and giving back."

__Rustin M. Lewis, DPA__ is a nonprofit executive, community leader, former political candidate, educator, and author. Reared in Gary, Indiana, Dr. Lewis was born into a family committed to volunteerism and community service. He has continued the Lewis family tradition by building a life and career dedicated to creating opportunities for the underserved.

Dr. Lewis is the executive director of Communities in Schools of the Nation's Capital. Previously, Dr. Lewis was a candidate in the 2018 At-Large DC Council race. Throughout his career, Dr. Lewis has served as a senior executive for local, regional, and national nonprofit organizations.

Dr. Lewis holds a doctorate in public administration from the University of Baltimore, a master of public administration degree, and a bachelor's degree in sociology from Clark Atlanta University. He also has executive management certificates from Harvard and Georgetown Universities.

Dr. Lewis is married to Renee Lewis, and they have a daughter, Reyna.

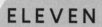

ELEVEN

FORGIVENESS

Chris Rey

From my relationship with my mother, I learned that forgiveness is a good deed. The act of forgiveness is a choice. My mother did drugs and other things that were not conducive to family life. She eventually got clean, built her life back, and put her old life in the past. Deep down inside, I knew the hurt and the pain that she felt because she had messed up. As her oldest child, I put my arms around her and decided to move on. I forgave her for not being a mother in the traditional sense. For me, it was the greatest good deed I have ever done. That good deed transformed my life, and my mother's life, as well. If I hadn't forgiven her, she might have continued to carry the hurt and the

shame she experienced. She may have relapsed. When I forgave her, she realized she had something to live for.

I didn't grow up with my mom or a dad. My grandmother and my uncle raised me. Uncle Jeth, who was about nineteen years old when he joined the military, wasn't that much older than me, but he took on the role of being my father figure because he understood that playing a role in my life would allow me to be successful. He poured everything he had into me. What my Uncle Jeth did for me was the greatest good deed that any man can do for a child.

My grandmother provided me with a strong foundation to serve people, always believing I would do amazing things. A very religious lady, we spent a lot of time in church, and the values instilled in me have served as the foundation for my giving and forgiving. Even though we didn't have much, we would volunteer at soup kitchens and homeless shelters, and feed the homeless long before I understood what we were doing. My community when I was growing up impacted my views on charity. Someone was always helping out, giving back, and opening up their hearts. Organizations or individuals gave away turkeys and boxes of food. The senior citizens on fixed incomes were helped. People who needed assistance paying their rent or light bills were also helped.

My grandmother also taught me that when God blessed me with an opportunity, I should be humble and remember the gifts I have are not to elevate me but be used to make life better for someone else or to change the trajectory of a life. Because of my grandmother, uncle, and even my mother, I have lived my entire adult life in the service of others.

The civil rights activist and congressman John Lewis was a huge inspiration to me. I remember he said to me, in his John Lewis voice, "Young brother, you're going to run for public office one day." I doubted it. "I'm never," I said, "running for public office." He said, "Oh, you will, and when you do, I'll be there." When I got to the point in my life where I was ready to run for office, I called John Lewis, and I told him I was running. He said he would be there to campaign, and he did. By holding true to his word, he turned it into a good deed. I ran for mayor three times, and he was there. I will never forget him for this. As mayor, I remembered the charity I saw in my growing years and implemented several service projects. I love to walk, and so I began the Walk with the Mayor Initiative. Being a senior citizen can be lonely, so I spent a lot of time at the senior center engaging our elders. For the Special Olympics, we spearheaded a torch run to raise funds. Our Fire Department made sure all the children in the community had a great Halloween.

As the president of Phi Beta Sigma fraternity, it is an honor and privilege to wake up every single day and lead thousands of my fraternity brothers from around the world. Service is the cornerstone of who we are as Sigma men. I provide inspiration and strategic direction and let them know what is possible when we roll up our sleeves and work for our community. As a fraternity, we are now building our first affordable housing complex. My hope is that putting a roof over a person's head will inspire the brotherhood to provide housing for generations to come.

GIFTS TO SELF

It is easy to be all about self, but it is hard to be there for other people, yet at times I feel I do too much. So I have found ways to give to myself. I have learned if I don't take time for me, nobody else will. I take time off, and I rest. I once took a couple of years off from leadership roles with Phi Beta Sigma because I needed to take a break and recharge. I also meditate in the mornings and try to do devotions daily. Meditation is my time to listen to God. Devotion is an opportunity for me to talk to God.

Chris V. Rey, JD, a native of St. Thomas, US Virgin Islands, was elected the thirty-sixth international president of Phi Beta Sigma Fraternity, Inc. at the 2021 International Conclave. Bro. Rey became a member of Phi Beta Sigma on the campus of East Carolina University in October 1996. He becomes the first member in the organization's 107-year history to rise to the rank of international president after serving as international first vice president and international second vice president, the highest collegiate leadership position in the fraternity. He has served at every level of the fraternity; most recently as international first vice president. Under his leadership, the fraternity broke membership growth records. As international director of social action, he was credited with the creation of the International Sigma Day of Service; as international technology director, he developed the first framework for the fraternity's membership database and technology infrastructure. At the age of twenty-seven, Brother Rey was elected one of the youngest regional directors in history, serving as the sixteenth southeastern regional director, providing oversight of North Carolina, South Carolina, and Eastern Tennessee membership. Brother Rey's campaign slogan, "B.E.L.I.E.V.E.," has been a clarion call to the membership. The crux of the message is that members must believe in their power and what is possible if they are united. "The next chapter will be our best yet," he said. "We will raise our engagement level to address poverty, access to the ballot box, the wealth gap, and health disparities for Black and brown men."

Brother Rey is deputy director of human resources for the US Army Materiel Command (AMC). AMC synchronizes and integrates the Army's total capabilities in support of the chief of staff of the army's priorities and Combatant Command requirements. As the Army's lead materiel integrator, AMC manages the global supply chain, synchronizing logistics and sustainment activities across the entire Army. Bro. Rey holds a bachelor of science degree in business administration and a juris doctor degree from William and Mary School of Law.

TWELVE

EDUCATIONAL
GOOD DEEDS

Dwight E. Rhodes

A colleague introduced me to a young person I'm mentoring who uses the pronoun "they." They are trying to start a school for queer students who do not feel welcomed in other spaces. All students would be welcomed, but the school would particularly be for queer students who do not feel welcomed in other spaces. We connect every two to three weeks for at least an hour. I'm not always dispensing pearls of wisdom, but I give my point of view. I listen to what they're saying and wrestling with. I offer the space for them to be more confident in themselves and to realize their voice is valuable, even in places where they are not welcomed.

I do this because when I worked as a chief academic officer in New Orleans after Hurricane Katrina, Dr. Edwin, an education consultant who served as one of the first Black principals of an all-White school in Boston in the 1950s, took me under his wing, molded me to be a better leader, nurtured me, and graciously gave his time, advice, and his generosity. Dr. Edwin wasn't gay—he was a married heterosexual man with three children—but he gave me the confidence to be even more proud of being Black and gay. He sensed that even at that stage of my life I still wasn't completely comfortable with myself and all of my identity markers. He would have conversations with me about leading with my full self and doing what other people thought I might not be able to achieve. He had graduated from Harvard University and encouraged me to apply to the doctoral program, although he couldn't guarantee I would get in. He gave this little Black boy from southern California, from very modest means, the audacity to apply to Harvard. Under his mentorship, I gained the confidence and direction I needed to finish my doctorate degree. The experience with Dr. Edwin inspires me to give back and to serve and support others.

When I was a first-year teacher, anyone could see my desk if they passed by my classroom. Beside my desk, I placed a couple of chairs. After a few weeks, students and adults would come to my classroom and sit in the chairs near my desk. We would engage in one-on-one conversations. It wasn't intentional, but I had developed a sort of therapist room and safe space where students and adults could feel comfortable. Both students and adults appreciated the chair beside my desk. People who walked by would tell me that the conversations always looked intriguing, engaging, and interesting. If the students were having a difficult time, they would come in even if I was in the middle of class and sit quietly in the chair for half the class. They would not disturb my class and would return to their class when they needed to. I did not know at the time that just by being there, when people needed me, I was mentoring.

During my last year of teaching, I had a student who had a lot of energy and always found himself in the middle of controversy. His mom was a single mom, and he had a younger sister. His mother knew he was a handful, and I distinctly remember her telling me to "beat his ass if you need to, Mr. Rhodes." I told her I couldn't do that. I spent a lot of time with this kid and sometimes I felt like I wasn't getting through to him or making progress. After I left the school and became a principal, we fell out of touch, but I heard that he finished school. About seven years later, I was living in another city and received a phone call from him. "You may not remember me," he said, "but I was your student in the eighth grade." You could have knocked me over with a feather! He had just accepted a position in that city as a chef. Prior to accepting the position, he had spent three and a half years studying in Paris.

There's intersectionality between education, doing good deeds, and giving—intersectionality between education and being charitable. I don't say "giving back" but "giving for the future." I give much of my time, energy, expertise, and skill-set. Some people say I need to monetize my time, but I do things from my heart because, for me, it's intangible things that I give. When I give my time, that's more valuable than money.

My partner and I moved from a metropolitan, progressive city to a Deep South town of about twenty-three thousand people that did not embrace my identity markers. We moved to provide direct support to my octogenarian parents. I'm Black. I'm gay. I'm married to an immigrant. I'm agnostic. Those identity markers are not embraced here. My partner and I knew we would pay a psychological and emotional toll. But every time I look out of my office window and see my mom and dad sitting out on the porch in their rocking chairs, not having a care in the world, I know it's worth it that I'm doing good deeds.

GIFTS TO SELF

An act of kindness is an act of kindness. There is no small or large act of kindness. I've learned it is important to be kind to yourself and to others. That's not always easy for me. There are times I have to say no and draw a line of demarcation, particularly when someone has an opposing ideology.

I've been in education for twenty-five years, and many of my colleagues have transitioned out and retired, but I feel that I still have a lot to learn and give. There's so much more for me in this crazy thing we call life.

*As CEO and founder of Rhodes2Equity Consulting, LLC (R2E), **Dwight E. Rhodes** courageously values putting students first—not politics, not profits. Dwight has a proven track record for providing equitable outcomes for students by dramatically improving their schools and districts. R2E is the intersection of his learning as a 2017 Harvard doctoral graduate of educational leadership and a twenty-plus-year educator. As the former chief transformation specialist for Georgia's ESSA Plan to transform its lowest-performing schools, Dwight was instrumental in transforming historically "F" schools into nearly "B" rated schools within two years. He and the Chief Turnaround Office Team transformed schools and districts by getting to the root of problems and removing barriers for district and school-level leaders. To achieve this, he implemented a design thinking framework that created the space for district and school leaders to utilize research, ideation, and prototyping to reimagine how to improve academic outcomes for all students, particularly students of color. Dwight has also served as CEO of a continuing education organization, Design Arts Seminars. In this role, he led the organization in its mission to "think outside*

---

the box" to increase student diversity in science, technology, engineering, arts, and mathematics (STEAM)-related fields. Previously, he served as the founding chief academic officer and chief advocacy officer (CAO) for ReNEW Schools Charter Management Organization. ReNEW Schools CMO successfully restarts the lowest-performing schools in New Orleans. With him as CAO, ReNEW Schools experienced an average increase of thirty points in its annual school performance scores. Prior educational experience also includes serving as director of innovative school reform, as an elementary school principal, and as a middle school teacher of the year.

ABOUT THE
AUTHORS

The chief executive officer of Bridge Philanthropic Consulting, Dwayne Ashley is renowned for his bold, strategic thinking and wise counsel in philanthropy. He is a successful entrepreneur who, throughout the course of his career, has raised more than one billion dollars. A fearless and authentic solicitor, he is committed to social justice and helping organizations of color maximize their fundraising success. He advises nonprofits, philanthropists, and influencers globally.

A powerhouse of energy with a passion for fundraising, Dwayne has managed capital and annual campaigns and spearheaded development for such notable organizations as Jazz at Lincoln Center, 100 Black Men

of America, the Thurgood Marshall College Fund, the United Negro College Fund, the United Way of Texas Gulf Coast, and many others.

Dwayne is a thought leader in the field of philanthropy and has shared valuable concepts in numerous articles and in four books. They include *Eight Steps to Raising Money: Measuring Your Fundraising Impact*; *Word for Word Publishing*; *8 Winning Steps to Creating a Successful Special Event* with Carol Campbell, director of events at Prairie View A&M University; *I'll Find a Way or Make One: A Tribute to HBCUs* with noted journalist Juan Williams; and *Dream Internships: It's Not Who You Know, But What You Know!* An alumnus of Wiley College and the University of Pennsylvania's Fel's School of Government, he is very proud of his great-grandmother's contribution of land to establish one of the oldest schools to educate Black people in Heflin, Louisiana. The school is now one of the oldest Black churches in the state of Louisiana.

A member of the Phi Beta Sigma Fraternity and the Association of Fundraising Professionals (AFP), Dwayne has served as a member of the boards of AFP in the Philadelphia and

New York chapters. He serves on the board of directors of the Giving Institute, African American Development Officers, and the New York Society Library. Dwayne is active in One Hundred Black Men of New York and the Phi Beta Sigma Fraternity.

Dwayne enjoys travel: "I have visited more than one hundred countries and bake a mean mac and cheese."

Ava Williams Muhammad is a writer and experienced fact-seeker with an allegiance to the truth. Ava's experience in editorial content for magazines and books has cultivated her fact-finding skills.

As a self-employed book researcher, Ava assisted writers by combing through archives, finding biographical information, quotes, books, and news articles for several *New York Times* best-selling books published by HarperCollins, MacMillan, and Penguin Random House.

As an acquisitions sourcing editor for the defunct tech book publisher Callisto Media, Ava crafted Boolean and web-based searches to identify potential authors for forthcoming titles.

Ava has worked full-time as a magazine research editor at *Marie Claire*, *Michigan Avenue*, *Aspen Peak*, *Hamptons*, and *Boston Common* magazines. She has freelanced fact-checked at *Allure*, *Essence*, and *InStyle*.

Ava's writing has been published in *Hamptons* magazine, *Black Issues Book Review*, and the *New York Beacon*. She contributed three entries to *The Greenwood Encyclopedia of Hip-Hop Literature*. She has attended fiction and novel writing classes at the Sackett Street Writers Workshop.

Ava was selected to attend the Minority Writers Seminar at the Freedom Forum Diversity Institute in Nashville, Tennessee. Ava mentored a high school student for two years as a volunteer with the iMentor program.

Ava holds a master's degree in publishing from Pace University and a bachelor's degree in English from Spelman College. As a graduate student at Pace, she was awarded a graduate fellowship. As an undergraduate, Ava was the recipient the summer minority research fellowship at Cornell University and the UNCF Arthur Ross Foundation scholarship. At Cornell, she researched the perceptions of dark-skinned and light-skinned Blacks in eighteenth and nineteenth century African American literature, and she presented her work at a leadership alliance conference in Washington, DC.

Ava is a collector of autographed books. Her collection includes books signed by Toni Morrison, Maya Angelou, Edwidge Danticat, and Zadie Smith. Brooklyn born with a strong appreciation for her Southern roots, Ava hopes to walk in the shadows of the literary artists she admires who have declared writing as their "write to life."